63 DAYS

OF

GRATITUDE

DAWN BOWERS

ISBN: 979-8-89572-005-9
www.mommyscribbles.com

Dedication

"And He said to me, "My grace is sufficient for you, for My strength is made perfect in weakness." Therefore most gladly I will rather boast in my infirmities, that the power of Christ may rest upon me."
2 Corinthians 12:9 NKJV

63 DAYS OF GRATITUDE

FORWARD

So I was standing at the kitchen sink washing my plate, getting ready for dinner and I remember hearing my teenage daughter whisper "Mommy I'm scared" for the hundredth time that day and instantly I felt that twinge of guilt that only a parent could feel...

You know that helpless feeling you get when you see your child struggling with something that you can't do anything about?

Well, little did I know that that moment would spur me on to going on a 21 day word fast followed by attending a 90 day novel writing class.

When I took that class everything changed. As I wrote my first novel (which I chose not to publish) I discovered a unique approach to breaking negative patterns of thought in order to have more peace which ultimately has changed my life and my children's lives…

In fact…that daughter who used to say "Mommy I'm scared" a hundred times a day…no longer clings to me in constant fear…no longer follows me around as if she's my shadow…

63 DAYS OF GRATITUDE

FORWARD CONT.

That daughter is now going off on her first mission's trip and wanting to go to Africa as a missionary when she graduates high school.

This is the power of positive thinking…

And in this book you will get a chance to discover the exact strategies that I used to help my family and I break negative thought patterns and have more peace.

I pray that you are blessed by these exercises as you allow God to work on you during these next 63 days.

Until Next Time,
Keep Asking, Keep Seeking, Keep Knocking,
AND
Keep Scribbling!

love Dawn

63 DAYS OF GRATITUDE

THE STRATEGY

You know that saying... "it takes 21 days to make or break a habit"?

Well they've done studies to prove that it actually takes 63 days for that habit to stick because the way we think **is** a habit.

It's like a computer program that gets stuck on repeat and becomes really hard to change.

So If we want to make a change to think more positive it's important to first become aware of how we think and notice how we act.

We need to start paying attention to how we feel in different situations, but we can't really do that if we aren't taking our thoughts captive.

This is easier said then done when we are just talking things out with our best friend or counselor. it's wonderful to seek counsel...

In fact the bible tells us to seek wise counsel, but we can often become lost in a sea of words if all we do is "talk it out".

63 DAYS OF GRATITUDE

THE STRATEGY

Before we get into the strategy though, if we want to truly break the loop of negative patterns of thought, it'll help if we can first think of our brains like a tree with lots of branches.

Imagine starting out in life with an amazing tree full of life and greenery, but as we experience different things we begin to feed on the positive and negative patterns of our family and other people around us.

Unfortunately the more negative things we experience early on in life the more negative things perpetuate in our lives…because perception is reality.

So with every negative, a branch dies and with every positive, a new branch grows.

Everything we experience, everything we hear…helps to shape our thoughts, but thank the Lord that we don't have to settle for what's right in front of us because of the way God has made our brains.

It's pretty fascinating, if you ask me, and very complex to understand, but studies have

63 DAYS OF GRATITUDE

THE STRATEGY

shown that hearing and seeing things is often not enough to break negative patterns of thought.

(Sorry to break it to you…but speaking positive affirmations is not enough…)

Dr. Carolynn Leafe says that in order to create new, healthy "branches", we NEED to write.

Writing creates a brain to hand connection that helps us actualize and internalize the new patterns of thought we are trying to implement.

This is an important strategy to use because oftentimes what we see and hear in our daily life does not reflect the healthy positive thoughts we want.

Often our life feels chaotic and negative and the saying "seeing is believing" becomes very concrete. So in order to combat this we need to pick up the pen and start writing…

The intricate details of our brains are pretty amazing, but I'm not going to sit here and

63 DAYS OF GRATITUDE

pretend I understand it.

What I do understand though is that I have Ginoscos…which in Greek basically means I have experiential knowledge.

I know the benefits of what writing has done for me first hand and when used correctly thoughts literally disentangle themselves as they pass through our fingertips.

With that being said though, there is a caveat…you have to write with a purpose and a plan…

Yes, journaling and writing whatever is on our heart is an important way to process our thoughts and feelings, **and we will do that in this book**, but if we're not replacing those thoughts with something good then nothing is going to change.

I could go more into this, but for the purpose of this book we are just going to focus on implementing the strategies that I used to help me and my family break those negative loops.

63 DAYS OF GRATITUDE

THE STRATEGY

On the following page I'm gonna give you the 5 steps you need to fully implement the strategies so you can experience the benefits for yourself.

So let's get ready to break those chains that have kept us bound and broken for far too long so we can finally have more peace.

BONUS AUDIO TRAINING

Need to relax and unwind after a hard day? Scan the QR code for a Free Guided Meditation on the Fruits of the Spirit so you can reset and focus on God's truth and being filled with the Holy Spirit.

HOW TO GET THE MOST OUT OF OF THIS JOURNAL

Step #1: Read 1 Proverb every day starting with Proverbs 1 on Day 1, Proverbs 2 Day 2, and so on. You will complete 2 rounds of Proverbs plus a couple of days by the time you finish this book.

Step #2: Practice the memory verse for the week (saying AND writing it is recommended).

Step #3: Each week you will be given a fruit of the spirit to focus on and each day you will have a writing prompt that gives you an opportunity to "step into the shoes" of that week's fruit of the spirit (think of the movie "Inside Out").

Step #4: Reflect weekly and look for any positive or negative patterns in your writing...Allow God to speak to you as different memories are spurred on with each prompt.

Step #5: Reflect on what your most grateful for during the week.

MEET THE AUTHOR

DAWN BOWERS
AUTHOR | HEALTH AND WELLNESS COACH

HELPING WOMEN OF FAITH REDUCE STRESS AND LIVE WELL SO THEY CAN GO FROM SURVIVING TO THRIVING NATURALLY.

This Is Me.

MEMORY VERSES

WEEKLY MEMORY VERSES

MEMORY VERSE WEEK 1

"NOT THAT I SPEAK IN REGARD FOR NEED FOR I HAVE LEARNED IN WHATEVER STATE I AM TO BE CONTENT..." PHILIPPIANS 4:11

MEMORY VERSE WEEK 2

"BUT NONE OF THESE THINGS MOVE ME, NOR DO I COUNT MY LIFE DEAR TO MYSELF SO THAT I MAY FINISH MY RACE WITH JOY AND THE MINISTRY THAT I RECEIVED FROM THE LORD JESUS TO TESTIFY TO THE GOSPEL OF THE GRACE OF GOD" ACTS 20:24

MEMORY VERSE WEEK 3

"THAT CHRIST MAY DWELL IN YOUR HEARTS THROUGH FAITH THAT YOU BEING ROOTED AND GROUNDED IN LOVE" EPHESIANS 3:17

MEMORY VERSE WEEK 4

"FOR BECAUSE HE HIMSELF HAS SUFFERED WHEN TEMPTED HE IS ABLE TO HELP THOSE WHO ARE BEING TEMPTED." HEBREWS 2:18

MEMORY VERSES

WEEKLY MEMORY VERSES

MEMORY VERSE WEEK 5

"BUT WE MUST HOLD ONTO THE PROGRESS
WE HAVE ALREADY MADE."
PHILIPPIANS 3:16

MEMORY VERSE WEEK 6

"DON'T WORRY ABOUT ANYTHING,
INSTEAD PRAY ABOUT
EVERYTHING, TELL GOD WHAT YOU
NEED AND THANK HIM FOR ALL HE
HAS DONE."
PHILIPPIANS 4:6

MEMORY VERSE WEEK 7

"FOR GOD DOES NOT GIVE US A
SPIRIT OF FEAR, BUT OF
POWER AND OF LOVE AND OF
SOUND MIND."
2 TIMOTHY 1:7

MEMORY VERSE WEEK 8

"AND WE HAVE KNOWN AND
BELIEVED THE LOVE THAT GOD HAS
FOR US. GOD IS LOVE, AND HE
WHO ABIDES IN LOVE ABIDES IN
GOD, AND GOD IN HIM."
1 JOHN 4:16

MEMORY VERSES

WEEKLY MEMORY VERSES

MEMORY VERSE WEEK 9

"FINALLY, BRETHREN, WHATEVER THINGS ARE TRUE, WHATEVER THINGS, ARE NOBLE, WHATEVER THINGS ARE JUST, WHATEVER THINGS ARE PURE, WHATEVER THINGS ARE LOVELY, WHATEVER THINGS ARE OF GOOD REPORT, IF THERE IS ANY VIRTUE, AND IF THERE IS ANYTHING PRAISEWORTHY, MEDITATE ON THESE THINGS."
PHILIPPIANS 4:8

WEEK 1

"Not that I speak in regard for need for I have learned in whatever state I am to be content..."
Philippians 4:11

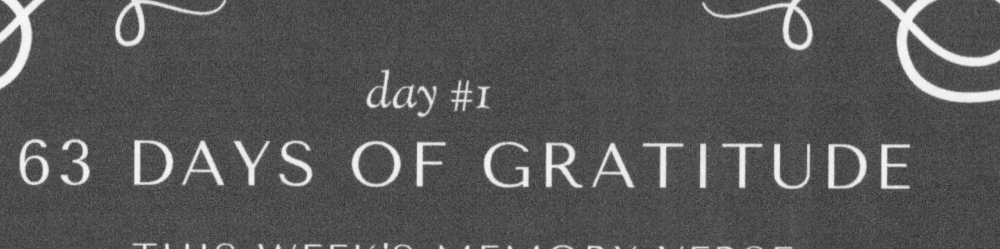

63 DAYS OF GRATITUDE

THIS WEEK'S MEMORY VERSE

"Not that I speak in regard for need for I have learned in whatever state I am to be content..."
Philippians 4:11

ONE THING THAT ANNOYED/FRUSTRATED ME TODAY...

_____

_____

_____

_____

_____

GOD, THANK YOU THAT...

_____

_____

_____

_____

_____

SPIRITUAL GROWTH PROMPT

This week pretend you are Love as if Love was a person
and for 5 minutes write as fast as you can starting with...

♥ ♥

"The most incredible thing I ever did was..."

day #2

63 DAYS OF GRATITUDE

THIS WEEK'S MEMORY VERSE

*"Not that I speak in regard for need for I have
learned in whatever state I am to be content..."*
Philippians 4:11

ONE THING THAT ANNOYED/FRUSTRATED ME TODAY...

_____
_____
_____
_____
_____
_____

GOD, THANK YOU THAT...

_____
_____
_____
_____
_____

SPIRITUAL GROWTH PROMPT

This week pretend you are Love as if Love was a person
and for 5 minutes write as fast as you can starting with...

♥ ♥

"If I had to describe myself I would say that I am..."

_____

_____

_____

_____

_____

_____

_____

_____

_____

_____

_____

_____

_____

63 DAYS OF GRATITUDE

THIS WEEK'S MEMORY VERSE

*"Not that I speak in regard for need for I have
learned in whatever state I am to be content..."*
Philippians 4:11

ONE THING THAT ANNOYED/FRUSTRATED ME TODAY...

_____
_____
_____
_____
_____
_____

GOD, THANK YOU THAT...

_____
_____
_____
_____
_____

SPIRITUAL GROWTH PROMPT

This week pretend you are Love as if Love was a person
and for 5 minutes write as fast as you can starting with...

♥ ♥

"The worst day of my life was when..."

_____

_____

_____

_____

_____

_____

_____

_____

_____

_____

_____

_____

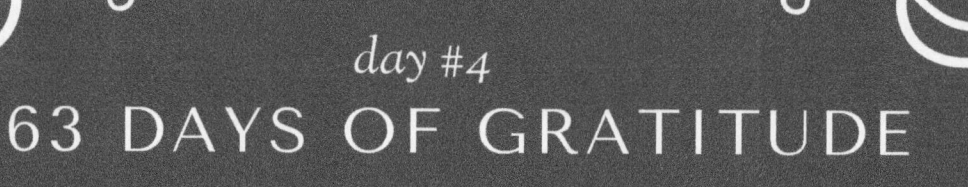

day #4
63 DAYS OF GRATITUDE
THIS WEEK'S MEMORY VERSE

"Not that I speak in regard for need for I have learned in whatever state I am to be content..."
Philippians 4:11

ONE THING THAT ANNOYED/FRUSTRATED ME TODAY...

_____
_____
_____
_____
_____
_____

GOD, THANK YOU THAT...

_____
_____
_____
_____
_____
_____

SPIRITUAL GROWTH PROMPT

This week pretend you are Love as if Love was a person
and for 5 minutes write as fast as you can starting with...

♥ ♥

"I need to be forgiven for..."

_____

_____

_____

_____

_____

_____

_____

_____

_____

_____

_____

_____

_____

_____

63 DAYS OF GRATITUDE

THIS WEEK'S MEMORY VERSE

*"Not that I speak in regard for need for I have
learned in whatever state I am to be content..."*
Philippians 4:11

ONE THING THAT ANNOYED/FRUSTRATED ME TODAY...

_____
_____
_____
_____
_____
_____

GOD, THANK YOU THAT...

_____
_____
_____
_____
_____

SPIRITUAL GROWTH PROMPT

This week pretend you are Love as if Love was a person
and for 5 minutes write as fast as you can starting with...

———————— ♥ ♥ ————————

"The turning point in my life was when..."

_____

_____

_____

_____

_____

_____

_____

_____

_____

_____

_____

_____

_____

63 DAYS OF GRATITUDE

THIS WEEK'S MEMORY VERSE

*"Not that I speak in regard for need for I have
learned in whatever state I am to be content..."*
Philippians 4:11

ONE THING THAT ANNOYED/FRUSTRATED ME TODAY...

_____

_____

_____

_____

_____

_____

GOD, THANK YOU THAT...

_____

_____

_____

_____

_____

SPIRITUAL GROWTH PROMPT

This week pretend you are Love as if Love was a person
and for 5 minutes write as fast as you can starting with...

♥ ♥

"Everything will make sense when..."

_____

_____

_____

_____

_____

_____

_____

_____

_____

_____

_____

_____

_____

63 DAYS OF GRATITUDE

THIS WEEK'S MEMORY VERSE

"Not that I speak in regard for need for I have learned in whatever state I am to be content..."
Philippians 4:11

ONE THING THAT ANNOYED/FRUSTRATED ME TODAY...

_____

_____

_____

_____

_____

_____

GOD, THANK YOU THAT...

_____

_____

_____

_____

_____

SPIRITUAL GROWTH PROMPT

This week pretend you are Love as if Love was a person
and for 5 minutes write as fast as you can starting with...

❤ ❤

"You would never know this by looking at me, but..."

_____

_____

_____

_____

_____

_____

_____

_____

_____

_____

_____

_____

_____

_____

TIME TO REFLECT
FIRST...DO YOU SEE ANY PATTERNS IN YOUR WRITING?

SECOND...WHAT ARE YOU MOST GRATEFUL FOR THIS WEEK?

WEEK 2

"But none of these things move me, nor do I count my life dear to myself so that I may finish my race with joy and the ministry that I received from the Lord Jesus to testify to the gospel of the grace of God."

Acts 20:24

63 DAYS OF GRATITUDE

THIS WEEK'S MEMORY VERSE

"But none of these things move me, nor do I count my life dear to myself so that I may finish my race with joy and the ministry that I received from the Lord Jesus to testify to the gospel of the grace of God"

Acts 20:24

ONE THING THAT ANNOYED/FRUSTRATED ME TODAY...

_____

_____

_____

_____

_____

_____

GOD, THANK YOU THAT...

_____

_____

_____

_____

_____

SPIRITUAL GROWTH PROMPT

This week pretend you are Joy as if Joy was a person and
for 5 minutes write as fast as you can starting with...

♥ ♥

"I like it when you ..."

_____

_____

_____

_____

_____

_____

_____

_____

_____

_____

_____

_____

_____

THIS WEEK'S MEMORY VERSE

"But none of these things move me, nor do I count my life dear to myself so that I may finish my race with joy and the ministry that I received from the Lord Jesus to testify to the gospel of the grace of God"
Acts 20:24

ONE THING THAT ANNOYED/FRUSTRATED ME TODAY...

_____

_____

_____

_____

_____

_____

GOD, THANK YOU THAT...

_____

_____

_____

_____

_____

_____

This week pretend you are Joy as if Joy was a person and
for 5 minutes write as fast as you can starting with...

♥ ♥

"You would never know this by looking at me, but..."

_____

_____

_____

_____

_____

_____

_____

_____

_____

_____

_____

_____

_____

_____

63 DAYS OF GRATITUDE

THIS WEEK'S MEMORY VERSE

*"But none of these things move me, nor do I count my life dear to myself
so that I may finish my race with joy and the ministry that I received
from the Lord Jesus to testify to the gospel of the grace of God"*
Acts 20:24

ONE THING THAT ANNOYED/FRUSTRATED ME
TODAY...

_____

_____

_____

_____

_____

_____

GOD, THANK YOU THAT...

_____

_____

_____

_____

_____

_____

SPIRITUAL GROWTH PROMPT

This week pretend you are Joy as if Joy was a person and
for 5 minutes write as fast as you can starting with...

♥ ♥

"I struggle with..."

day #11
63 DAYS OF GRATITUDE

THIS WEEK'S MEMORY VERSE

"But none of these things move me, nor do I count my life dear to myself so that I may finish my race with joy and the ministry that I received from the Lord Jesus to testify to the gospel of the grace of God"
Acts 20:24

ONE THING THAT ANNOYED/FRUSTRATED ME TODAY...

_____

_____

_____

_____

_____

_____

GOD, THANK YOU THAT...

_____

_____

_____

_____

_____

SPIRITUAL GROWTH PROMPT

This week pretend you are Joy as if Joy was a person and
for 5 minutes write as fast as you can starting with...

♥ ♥

"I cannot allow..."

63 DAYS OF GRATITUDE

THIS WEEK'S MEMORY VERSE

*"But none of these things move me, nor do I count my life dear to myself
so that I may finish my race with joy and the ministry that I received
from the Lord Jesus to testify to the gospel of the grace of God"*
Acts 20:24

ONE THING THAT ANNOYED/FRUSTRATED ME TODAY...

_____

_____

_____

_____

_____

_____

GOD, THANK YOU THAT...

_____

_____

_____

_____

_____

SPIRITUAL GROWTH PROMPT

This week pretend you are Joy as if Joy was a person and
for 5 minutes write as fast as you can starting with...

♥ ♥

"I'm beginning to question why I..."

_____

_____

_____

_____

_____

_____

_____

_____

_____

_____

_____

_____

_____

_____

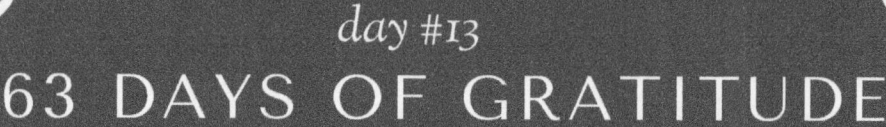

63 DAYS OF GRATITUDE

THIS WEEK'S MEMORY VERSE

*"But none of these things move me, nor do I count my life dear to myself
so that I may finish my race with joy and the ministry that I received
from the Lord Jesus to testify to the gospel of the grace of God"*
Acts 20:24

ONE THING THAT ANNOYED/FRUSTRATED ME TODAY...

_____

_____

_____

_____

_____

_____

GOD, THANK YOU THAT...

_____

_____

_____

_____

_____

This week pretend you are Joy as if Joy was a person and
for 5 minutes write as fast as you can starting with...

♥ ♥

"One thing you still need to know about me is..."

_____

_____

_____

_____

_____

_____

_____

_____

_____

_____

_____

_____

_____

_____

THIS WEEK'S MEMORY VERSE

"But none of these things move me, nor do I count my life dear to myself so that I may finish my race with joy and the ministry that I received from the Lord Jesus to testify to the gospel of the grace of God"
Acts 20:24

ONE THING THAT ANNOYED/FRUSTRATED ME TODAY...

_____

_____

_____

_____

_____

_____

GOD, THANK YOU THAT...

_____

_____

_____

_____

_____

This week pretend you are Joy as if Joy was a person and
for 5 minutes write as fast as you can starting with...

♥ ♥

"My parents think I'm..."

_____

_____

_____

_____

_____

_____

_____

_____

_____

_____

_____

_____

_____

TIME TO REFLECT
FIRST...DO YOU SEE ANY PATTERNS IN YOUR WRITING?

SECOND...WHAT ARE YOU MOST GRATEFUL FOR THIS WEEK?

WEEK 3

"That Christ may dwell in your hearts through faith that you being rooted and grounded in love"
Ephesians 3:17

63 DAYS OF GRATITUDE

THIS WEEK'S MEMORY VERSE

"That Christ may dwell in your hearts through faith that you being rooted and grounded in love"
Ephesians 3:17

ONE THING THAT ANNOYED/FRUSTRATED ME TODAY...

_____

_____

_____

_____

_____

_____

GOD, THANK YOU THAT...

_____

_____

_____

_____

_____

SPIRITUAL GROWTH PROMPT

This week pretend you are Peace as if Peace was a person and for 5 minutes write as fast as you can starting with...

———————— ♥ ♥ ————————

"Every time I think I'm going to get what I want, it seems that..."

_____

_____

_____

_____

_____

_____

_____

_____

_____

_____

_____

_____

_____

day #16

63 DAYS OF GRATITUDE

THIS WEEK'S MEMORY VERSE

"That Christ may dwell in your hearts through faith that you being rooted and grounded in love"
Ephesians 3:17

ONE THING THAT ANNOYED/FRUSTRATED ME TODAY...

_____

_____

_____

_____

_____

_____

GOD, THANK YOU THAT...

_____

_____

_____

_____

_____

SPIRITUAL GROWTH PROMPT

This week pretend you are Peace as if Peace was a person and for 5 minutes write as fast as you can starting with...

❤ ❤

"The thing that people admire most about me is..."

_____

_____

_____

_____

_____

_____

_____

_____

_____

_____

_____

_____

_____

63 DAYS OF GRATITUDE

THIS WEEK'S MEMORY VERSE

*"That Christ may dwell in your hearts through faith that you being
rooted and grounded in love"*
Ephesians 3:17

ONE THING THAT ANNOYED/FRUSTRATED ME
TODAY...

_____

_____

_____

_____

_____

GOD, THANK YOU THAT...

_____

_____

_____

_____

SPIRITUAL GROWTH PROMPT

This week pretend you are Peace as if Peace was a person and for 5 minutes write as fast as you can starting with...

♥ ♥

"The characteristic I'm least proud of in myself is..."

_____

_____

_____

_____

_____

_____

_____

_____

_____

_____

_____

_____

_____

63 DAYS OF GRATITUDE

THIS WEEK'S MEMORY VERSE

"That Christ may dwell in your hearts through faith that you being rooted and grounded in love"
Ephesians 3:17

ONE THING THAT ANNOYED/FRUSTRATED ME
TODAY...

_____
_____
_____
_____
_____
_____

GOD, THANK YOU THAT...

_____
_____
_____
_____
_____

SPIRITUAL GROWTH PROMPT

This week pretend you are Peace as if Peace was a person and for 5 minutes write as fast as you can starting with...

♥ ♥

"I pretend to have forgotten about the time that..."

_____

_____

_____

_____

_____

_____

_____

_____

_____

_____

_____

_____

_____

_____

63 DAYS OF GRATITUDE

THIS WEEK'S MEMORY VERSE

"That Christ may dwell in your hearts through faith that you being rooted and grounded in love"
Ephesians 3:17

ONE THING THAT ANNOYED/FRUSTRATED ME TODAY...

_____

_____

_____

_____

_____

GOD, THANK YOU THAT...

_____

_____

_____

_____

_____

SPIRITUAL GROWTH PROMPT

This week pretend you are Peace as if Peace was a person and for 5 minutes write as fast as you can starting with...

♥ ♥

"The answer to my problem that I've been avoiding is..."

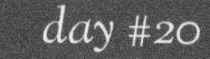

63 DAYS OF GRATITUDE

THIS WEEK'S MEMORY VERSE

"That Christ may dwell in your hearts through faith that you being rooted and grounded in love"
Ephesians 3:17

ONE THING THAT ANNOYED/FRUSTRATED ME TODAY...

_____
_____
_____
_____
_____
_____

GOD, THANK YOU THAT...

_____
_____
_____
_____
_____

SPIRITUAL GROWTH PROMPT

This week pretend you are Peace as if Peace was a person and for 5 minutes write as fast as you can starting with...

—————— ❤ ❤ ——————

"If I could do one thing differently from my past, it would be..."

_____

_____

_____

_____

_____

_____

_____

_____

_____

_____

_____

_____

_____

_____

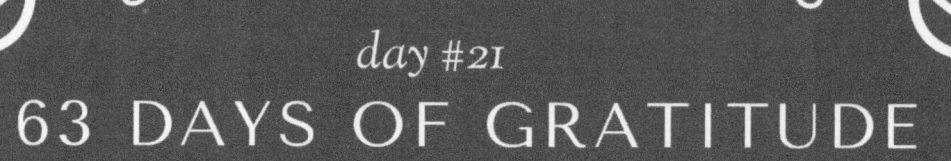

63 DAYS OF GRATITUDE

THIS WEEK'S MEMORY VERSE

"That Christ may dwell in your hearts through faith that you being rooted and grounded in love"
Ephesians 3:17

ONE THING THAT ANNOYED/FRUSTRATED ME TODAY...

_____

_____

_____

_____

_____

_____

GOD, THANK YOU THAT...

_____

_____

_____

_____

_____

_____

SPIRITUAL GROWTH PROMPT

This week pretend you are Peace as if Peace was a person and for 5
minutes write as fast as you can starting with...

❤

"I wouldn't be surprised if one day I..."

TIME TO REFLECT
FIRST...DO YOU SEE ANY PATTERNS IN YOUR WRITING?

SECOND...WHAT ARE YOU MOST GRATEFUL FOR THIS WEEK?

WEEK 4

"For because He himself has suffered when tempted he is able to help those who are being tempted."
Hebrews 2:18

day #22

63 DAYS OF GRATITUDE

THIS WEEK'S MEMORY VERSE

"For because He himself has suffered when tempted he is able to help those who are being tempted."
Hebrews 2:18

ONE THING THAT ANNOYED/FRUSTRATED ME TODAY...

_____

_____

_____

_____

_____

_____

GOD, THANK YOU THAT...

_____

_____

_____

_____

_____

This week pretend you are Patience as if Patience was a person
and for 5 minutes write as fast as you can starting with...

❤ ❤

"I tend to pretend that I..."

_____

_____

_____

_____

_____

_____

_____

_____

_____

_____

_____

_____

_____

_____

_____

63 DAYS OF GRATITUDE

THIS WEEK'S MEMORY VERSE

"For because He himself has suffered when tempted he is able to help those who are being tempted."
Hebrews 2:18

ONE THING THAT ANNOYED/FRUSTRATED ME TODAY...

_____
_____
_____
_____
_____
_____

GOD, THANK YOU THAT...

_____
_____
_____
_____
_____

SPIRITUAL GROWTH PROMPT

This week pretend you are Patience as if Patience was a person
and for 5 minutes write as fast as you can starting with...

♥ ♥

"The most challenging moment of my life was when I..."

_____

_____

_____

_____

_____

_____

_____

_____

_____

_____

_____

_____

_____

_____

_____

63 DAYS OF GRATITUDE

THIS WEEK'S MEMORY VERSE

"For because He himself has suffered when tempted he is able to help those who are being tempted."
Hebrews 2:18

ONE THING THAT ANNOYED/FRUSTRATED ME TODAY...

_____

_____

_____

_____

_____

_____

GOD, THANK YOU THAT...

_____

_____

_____

_____

_____

_____

This week pretend you are Patience as if Patience was a person and for 5 minutes write as fast as you can starting with...

───────── ♥ ♥ ─────────

"The most defiant moment of my life was when I..."

_____

_____

_____

_____

_____

_____

_____

_____

_____

_____

_____

_____

_____

_____

63 DAYS OF GRATITUDE

THIS WEEK'S MEMORY VERSE

"For because He himself has suffered when tempted he is able to help those who are being tempted."
Hebrews 2:18

ONE THING THAT ANNOYED/FRUSTRATED ME TODAY...

_____

_____

_____

_____

_____

_____

GOD, THANK YOU THAT...

_____

_____

_____

_____

_____

SPIRITUAL GROWTH PROMPT

This week pretend you are Patience as if Patience was a person
and for 5 minutes write as fast as you can starting with...

♥ ♥

"The bravest thing I've ever done is..."

_____

_____

_____

_____

_____

_____

_____

_____

_____

_____

_____

_____

day #26
63 DAYS OF GRATITUDE
THIS WEEK'S MEMORY VERSE

"For because He himself has suffered when tempted he is able to help those who are being tempted."
Hebrews 2:18

ONE THING THAT ANNOYED/FRUSTRATED ME TODAY...

_____
_____
_____
_____
_____
_____

GOD, THANK YOU THAT...

_____
_____
_____
_____
_____

SPIRITUAL GROWTH PROMPT

This week pretend you are Patience as if Patience was a person
and for 5 minutes write as fast as you can starting with...

❤ ❥

"The greatest sacrifice my mother ever did for me was..."

63 DAYS OF GRATITUDE

THIS WEEK'S MEMORY VERSE

"For because He himself has suffered when tempted he is able to help those who are being tempted."
Hebrews 2:18

ONE THING THAT ANNOYED/FRUSTRATED ME TODAY...

_____
_____
_____
_____
_____
_____

GOD, THANK YOU THAT...

_____
_____
_____
_____
_____

SPIRITUAL GROWTH PROMPT

This week pretend you are Patience as if Patience was a person
and for 5 minutes write as fast as you can starting with...

♥ ♥

"The most cowardly thing I've ever done is..."

_____

_____

_____

_____

_____

_____

_____

_____

_____

_____

_____

_____

_____

_____

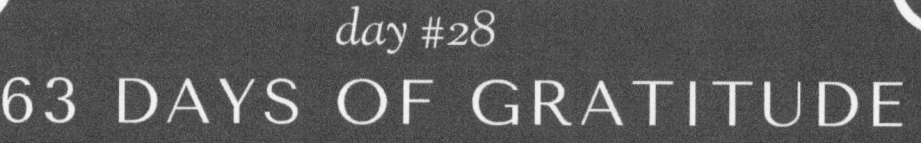

day #28

63 DAYS OF GRATITUDE

THIS WEEK'S MEMORY VERSE

"For because He himself has suffered when tempted he is able to help those who are being tempted."
Hebrews 2:18

ONE THING THAT ANNOYED/FRUSTRATED ME TODAY...

_____

_____

_____

_____

_____

GOD, THANK YOU THAT...

_____

_____

_____

_____

SPIRITUAL GROWTH PROMPT

This week pretend you are Patience as if Patience was a person
and for 5 minutes write as fast as you can starting with...

———————— ♥ ♥ ————————

"Justice will be done when..."

_____

_____

_____

_____

_____

_____

_____

_____

_____

_____

_____

_____

_____

_____

TIME TO REFLECT
FIRST...DO YOU SEE ANY PATTERNS IN YOUR WRITING?

_____

_____

_____

_____

_____

_____

SECOND...WHAT ARE YOU MOST GRATEFUL FOR THIS WEEK?

_____

_____

_____

_____

_____

_____

WEEK 5

"But we must hold onto the progress we have already made."
Philippians 3:16

day #29
63 DAYS OF GRATITUDE
THIS WEEK'S MEMORY VERSE

"But we must hold onto the progress we have already made."
Philippians 3:16

ONE THING THAT ANNOYED/FRUSTRATED ME
TODAY...

_____

_____

_____

_____

_____

_____

GOD, THANK YOU THAT...

_____

_____

_____

_____

_____

This week pretend you are Kindness as if Kindness was a person
and for 5 minutes write as fast as you can starting with...

♥ ♥

"The greatest thing my father ever gave up for me was..."

_____

_____

_____

_____

_____

_____

_____

_____

_____

_____

_____

_____

ONE THING THAT ANNOYED/FRUSTRATED ME TODAY...

_____

_____

_____

_____

_____

_____

GOD, THANK YOU THAT...

_____

_____

_____

_____

_____

SPIRITUAL GROWTH PROMPT

This week pretend you are Kindness as if Kindness was a person
and for 5 minutes write as fast as you can starting with...

♥ ♥

"I feel joyful when..."

day #31
63 DAYS OF GRATITUDE

THIS WEEK'S MEMORY VERSE

"But we must hold onto the progress we have already made."
Philippians 3:16

ONE THING THAT ANNOYED/FRUSTRATED ME TODAY...

_____

_____

_____

_____

_____

_____

GOD, THANK YOU THAT...

_____

_____

_____

_____

_____

SPIRITUAL GROWTH PROMPT

This week pretend you are Kindness as if Kindness was a person
and for 5 minutes write as fast as you can starting with...

——————— ❤ ❤ ———————

"I long for..."

_____

_____

_____

_____

_____

_____

_____

_____

_____

_____

_____

_____

63 DAYS OF GRATITUDE

THIS WEEK'S MEMORY VERSE

"But we must hold onto the progress we have already made."
Philippians 3:16

ONE THING THAT ANNOYED/FRUSTRATED ME TODAY...

_____

_____

_____

_____

_____

_____

GOD, THANK YOU THAT...

_____

_____

_____

_____

_____

This week pretend you are Kindness as if Kindness was a person
and for 5 minutes write as fast as you can starting with...

♥ ♥

"It breaks my heart when..."

_____

_____

_____

_____

_____

_____

_____

_____

_____

_____

_____

_____

_____

_____

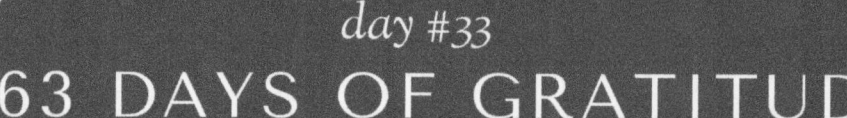

63 DAYS OF GRATITUDE

THIS WEEK'S MEMORY VERSE

"But we must hold onto the progress we have already made."
Philippians 3:16

ONE THING THAT ANNOYED/FRUSTRATED ME
TODAY...

_____

_____

_____

_____

_____

_____

GOD, THANK YOU THAT...

_____

_____

_____

_____

_____

_____

SPIRITUAL GROWTH PROMPT

This week pretend you are Kindness as if Kindness was a person
and for 5 minutes write as fast as you can starting with...

♥ ♥

"It makes me so angry when..."

_____

_____

_____

_____

_____

_____

_____

_____

_____

_____

_____

_____

_____

_____

63 DAYS OF GRATITUDE

THIS WEEK'S MEMORY VERSE

"But we must hold onto the progress we have already made."
Philippians 3:16

ONE THING THAT ANNOYED/FRUSTRATED ME
TODAY...

_____

_____

_____

_____

_____

_____

GOD, THANK YOU THAT...

_____

_____

_____

_____

_____

_____

SPIRITUAL GROWTH PROMPT

This week pretend you are Kindness as if Kindness was a person
and for 5 minutes write as fast as you can starting with...

♥ ♥

"I don't believe in..."

_____

_____

_____

_____

_____

_____

_____

_____

_____

_____

_____

_____

_____

63 DAYS OF GRATITUDE
THIS WEEK'S MEMORY VERSE

"But we must hold onto the progress we have already made."
Philippians 3:16

ONE THING THAT ANNOYED/FRUSTRATED ME
TODAY...

GOD, THANK YOU THAT...

SPIRITUAL GROWTH PROMPT

This week pretend you are Kindness as if Kindness was a person
and for 5 minutes write as fast as you can starting with...

♥ ♥

"I foolishly expect..."

_____

_____

_____

_____

_____

_____

_____

_____

_____

_____

_____

_____

_____

TIME TO REFLECT
FIRST...DO YOU SEE ANY PATTERNS IN YOUR WRITING?

_____

_____

_____

_____

_____

_____

_____

SECOND...WHAT ARE YOU MOST GRATEFUL FOR THIS WEEK?

_____

_____

_____

_____

_____

_____

WEEK 6

"Don't worry about anything, instead pray about everything, tell God what you need and thank Him for all He has done."
Philippians 4:6

63 DAYS OF GRATITUDE

THIS WEEK'S MEMORY VERSE

"Don't worry about anything, instead pray about everything, tell God what you need and thank Him for all He has done."
Philippians 4:6

ONE THING THAT ANNOYED/FRUSTRATED ME TODAY...

_____
_____
_____
_____
_____
_____

GOD, THANK YOU THAT...

_____
_____
_____
_____
_____

This week pretend you are Goodness as if Goodness was a person
and for 5 minutes write as fast as you can starting with...

♥ ♥

"I'm far too understanding..."

_____

_____

_____

_____

_____

_____

_____

_____

_____

_____

_____

_____

_____

63 DAYS OF GRATITUDE

THIS WEEK'S MEMORY VERSE

*"Don't worry about anything, instead pray about everything, tell God
what you need and thank Him for all He has done."*
Philippians 4:6

ONE THING THAT ANNOYED/FRUSTRATED ME TODAY...

_____

_____

_____

_____

_____

_____

GOD, THANK YOU THAT...

_____

_____

_____

_____

_____

_____

This week pretend you are Goodness as if Goodness was a person
and for 5 minutes write as fast as you can starting with...

♥ ♥

"I'm happiest when..."

_____

_____

_____

_____

_____

_____

_____

_____

_____

_____

_____

_____

_____

_____

THIS WEEK'S MEMORY VERSE

"Don't worry about anything, instead pray about everything, tell God what you need and thank Him for all He has done."
Philippians 4:6

ONE THING THAT ANNOYED/FRUSTRATED ME TODAY...

_____
_____
_____
_____
_____
_____

GOD, THANK YOU THAT...

_____
_____
_____
_____
_____

SPIRITUAL GROWTH PROMPT

This week pretend you are Goodness as if Goodness was a person and
for 5 minutes write as fast as you can starting with...

♥ ♥

"Something I've always wanted to say, but don't feel I'm allowed is..."

_____

_____

_____

_____

_____

_____

_____

_____

_____

_____

_____

_____

_____

_____

_____

63 DAYS OF GRATITUDE

THIS WEEK'S MEMORY VERSE

"Don't worry about anything, instead pray about everything, tell God what you need and thank Him for all He has done."
Philippians 4:6

ONE THING THAT ANNOYED/FRUSTRATED ME TODAY...

_____
_____
_____
_____
_____
_____

GOD, THANK YOU THAT...

_____
_____
_____
_____
_____

SPIRITUAL GROWTH PROMPT

This week pretend you are Goodness as if Goodness was a person and
for 5 minutes write as fast as you can starting with...

♥ ♥

"I would never..."

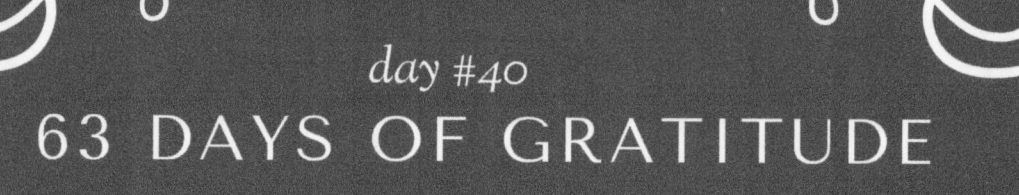

63 DAYS OF GRATITUDE

THIS WEEK'S MEMORY VERSE

*"Don't worry about anything, instead pray about everything, tell God
what you need and thank Him for all He has done."*
Philippians 4:6

ONE THING THAT ANNOYED/FRUSTRATED ME TODAY...

_____

_____

_____

_____

_____

_____

GOD, THANK YOU THAT...

_____

_____

_____

_____

_____

_____

SPIRITUAL GROWTH PROMPT

This week pretend you are Goodness as if Goodness was a person and
for 5 minutes write as fast as you can starting with...

——————————— ♥ ♥ ———————————

"I'm afraid of..."

63 DAYS OF GRATITUDE

THIS WEEK'S MEMORY VERSE

"Don't worry about anything, instead pray about everything, tell God what you need and thank Him for all He has done."
Philippians 4:6

ONE THING THAT ANNOYED/FRUSTRATED ME TODAY...

_____
_____
_____
_____
_____
_____

GOD, THANK YOU THAT...

_____
_____
_____
_____
_____
_____

This week pretend you are Goodness as if Goodness was a person and
for 5 minutes write as fast as you can starting with...

♥ ♥

"I have trouble saying yes when it comes to..."

_____

_____

_____

_____

_____

_____

_____

_____

_____

_____

_____

_____

_____

_____

"Don't worry about anything, instead pray about everything, tell God what you need and thank Him for all He has done."
Philippians 4:6

ONE THING THAT ANNOYED/FRUSTRATED ME TODAY...

_____

_____

_____

_____

_____

_____

GOD, THANK YOU THAT...

_____

_____

_____

_____

_____

_____

SPIRITUAL GROWTH PROMPT

This week pretend you are Goodness as if Goodness was a person and for 5 minutes write as fast as you can starting with...

♥ ♥

"I really regret..."

_____

_____

_____

_____

_____

_____

_____

_____

_____

_____

_____

_____

_____

_____

_____

_____

TIME TO REFLECT
FIRST...DO YOU SEE ANY PATTERNS IN YOUR WRITING?

SECOND...WHAT ARE YOU MOST GRATEFUL FOR THIS WEEK?

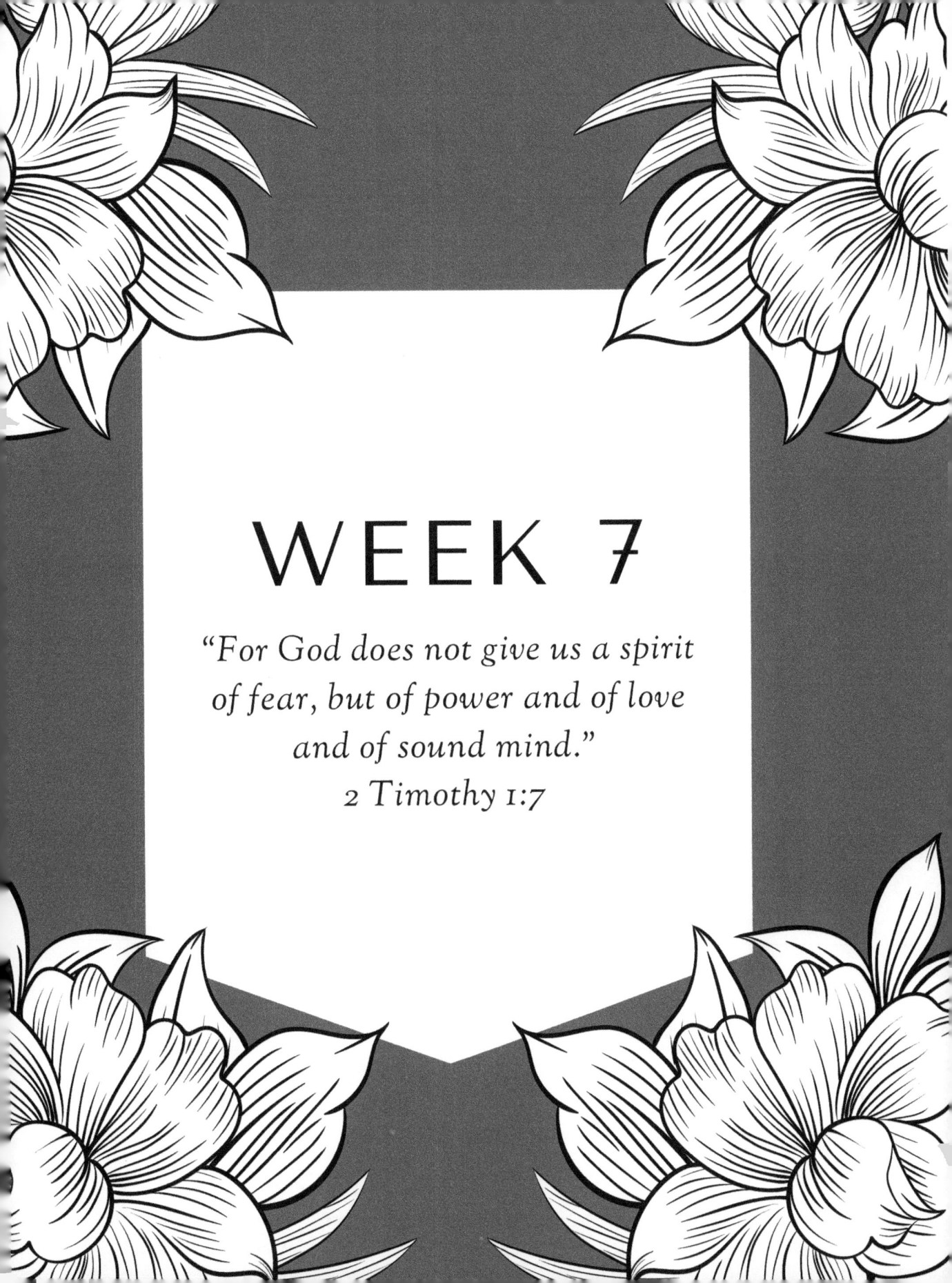

WEEK 7

"For God does not give us a spirit of fear, but of power and of love and of sound mind."
2 Timothy 1:7

63 DAYS OF GRATITUDE

THIS WEEK'S MEMORY VERSE

"For God does not give us a spirit of fear, but of power and of love and of sound mind."
2 Timothy 1:7

ONE THING THAT ANNOYED/FRUSTRATED ME TODAY...

_____
_____
_____
_____
_____
_____

GOD, THANK YOU THAT...

_____
_____
_____
_____
_____
_____

SPIRITUAL GROWTH PROMPT

This week pretend you are Faithfulness as if Faithfulness was a person
and for 5 minutes write as fast as you can starting with...

❤ ❤

"My best friend is..."

63 DAYS OF GRATITUDE

THIS WEEK'S MEMORY VERSE

"For God does not give us a spirit of fear, but of power and of love and of sound mind."
2 Timothy 1:7

ONE THING THAT ANNOYED/FRUSTRATED ME TODAY...

_____
_____
_____
_____
_____
_____

GOD, THANK YOU THAT...

_____
_____
_____
_____
_____
_____

SPIRITUAL GROWTH PROMPT

This week pretend you are Faithfulness as if Faithfulness was a person
and for 5 minutes write as fast as you can starting with...

"Never have I ever..."

_____

_____

_____

_____

_____

_____

_____

_____

_____

_____

_____

_____

_____

_____

"For God does not give us a spirit of fear, but of power and of love and of sound mind."
2 Timothy 1:7

ONE THING THAT ANNOYED/FRUSTRATED ME TODAY...

_____

_____

_____

_____

_____

GOD, THANK YOU THAT...

_____

_____

_____

_____

_____

SPIRITUAL GROWTH PROMPT

This week pretend you are Faithfulness as if Faithfulness was a person
and for 5 minutes write as fast as you can starting with...

————————— ❤ ❤ —————————

"One day I will..."

_____

_____

_____

_____

_____

_____

_____

_____

_____

_____

_____

_____

_____

63 DAYS OF GRATITUDE

THIS WEEK'S MEMORY VERSE

"For God does not give us a spirit of fear, but of power and of love and of sound mind."
2 Timothy 1:7

ONE THING THAT ANNOYED/FRUSTRATED ME TODAY...

_____

_____

_____

_____

_____

GOD, THANK YOU THAT...

_____

_____

_____

_____

_____

SPIRITUAL GROWTH PROMPT

This week pretend you are Faithfulness as if Faithfulness was a person
and for 5 minutes write as fast as you can starting with...

♥ ♥

"My worst enemy is..."

_____

_____

_____

_____

_____

_____

_____

_____

_____

_____

_____

_____

_____

_____

_____

63 DAYS OF GRATITUDE

THIS WEEK'S MEMORY VERSE

"For God does not give us a spirit of fear, but of power and of love and of sound mind."
2 Timothy 1:7

ONE THING THAT ANNOYED/FRUSTRATED ME
TODAY...

_____

_____

_____

_____

_____

_____

GOD, THANK YOU THAT...

_____

_____

_____

_____

_____

SPIRITUAL GROWTH PROMPT

This week pretend you are Faithfulness as if Faithfulness was a person
and for 5 minutes write as fast as you can starting with...

—————— ♥ ♥ ——————

"I wonder why..."

63 DAYS OF GRATITUDE

THIS WEEK'S MEMORY VERSE

"For God does not give us a spirit of fear, but of power and of love and of sound mind."
2 Timothy 1:7

ONE THING THAT ANNOYED/FRUSTRATED ME TODAY...

_____

_____

_____

_____

_____

_____

GOD, THANK YOU THAT...

_____

_____

_____

_____

_____

_____

SPIRITUAL GROWTH PROMPT

This week pretend you are Faithfulness as if Faithfulness was a person
and for 5 minutes write as fast as you can starting with...

———————— ♥ ♥ ————————

"When I'm afraid I tend to..."

63 DAYS OF GRATITUDE

THIS WEEK'S MEMORY VERSE

"For God does not give us a spirit of fear, but of power and of love and of sound mind."
2 Timothy 1:7

ONE THING THAT ANNOYED/FRUSTRATED ME TODAY...

_____
_____
_____
_____
_____
_____

GOD, THANK YOU THAT...

_____
_____
_____
_____
_____

SPIRITUAL GROWTH PROMPT

This week pretend you are Faithfulness as if Faithfulness was a person
and for 5 minutes write as fast as you can starting with...

❤ ❤

"My favorite thing to do is..."

TIME TO REFLECT
FIRST...DO YOU SEE ANY PATTERNS IN YOUR WRITING?

SECOND...WHAT ARE YOU MOST GRATEFUL FOR THIS WEEK?

WEEK 8

"And we have known and believed the love that God has for us. God is love, and he who abides in love abides in God, and God in him."
1 John 4:16

63 DAYS OF GRATITUDE

THIS WEEK'S MEMORY VERSE

"And we have known and believed the love that God has for us. God is love, and he who abides in love abides in God, and God in him."
1 John 4:16

ONE THING THAT ANNOYED/FRUSTRATED ME TODAY...

_____

_____

_____

_____

_____

_____

GOD, THANK YOU THAT...

_____

_____

_____

_____

_____

SPIRITUAL GROWTH PROMPT

This week pretend you are Gentleness as if Gentleness was a person and for 5 minutes write as fast as you can starting with...

♥ ♥

"I fear that when people look at me they see..."

_____

_____

_____

_____

_____

_____

_____

_____

_____

_____

_____

_____

_____

_____

63 DAYS OF GRATITUDE

THIS WEEK'S MEMORY VERSE

"And we have known and believed the love that God has for us. God is love, and he who abides in love abides in God, and God in him."
1 John 4:16

ONE THING THAT ANNOYED/FRUSTRATED ME TODAY...

_____

_____

_____

_____

_____

_____

GOD, THANK YOU THAT...

_____

_____

_____

_____

_____

_____

SPIRITUAL GROWTH PROMPT

This week pretend you are Gentleness as if Gentleness was a person and
for 5 minutes write as fast as you can starting with...

❤ ❤

"Sometimes when I'm alone I like to..."

_____

_____

_____

_____

_____

_____

_____

_____

_____

_____

_____

_____

_____

_____

63 DAYS OF GRATITUDE

THIS WEEK'S MEMORY VERSE

"And we have known and believed the love that God has for us. God is love, and he who abides in love abides in God, and God in him."
1 John 4:16

ONE THING THAT ANNOYED/FRUSTRATED ME TODAY...

_____

_____

_____

_____

_____

_____

GOD, THANK YOU THAT...

_____

_____

_____

_____

_____

This week pretend you are Gentleness as if Gentleness was a person and for 5 minutes write as fast as you can starting with...

♥ ♥

"My dream is to..."

63 DAYS OF GRATITUDE

THIS WEEK'S MEMORY VERSE

"And we have known and believed the love that God has for us. God is love, and he who abides in love abides in God, and God in him."
1 John 4:16

ONE THING THAT ANNOYED/FRUSTRATED ME TODAY...

_____
_____
_____
_____
_____
_____

GOD, THANK YOU THAT...

_____
_____
_____
_____
_____
_____

SPIRITUAL GROWTH PROMPT

This week pretend you are Gentleness as if Gentleness was a person and for 5 minutes write as fast as you can starting with...

♥ ♥

"My perfect day would be..."

_____

_____

_____

_____

_____

_____

_____

_____

_____

_____

_____

_____

_____

_____

63 DAYS OF GRATITUDE

THIS WEEK'S MEMORY VERSE

"And we have known and believed the love that God has for us. God is love, and he who abides in love abides in God, and God in him."
1 John 4:16

ONE THING THAT ANNOYED/FRUSTRATED ME TODAY...

_____
_____
_____
_____
_____
_____

GOD, THANK YOU THAT...

_____
_____
_____
_____
_____

SPIRITUAL GROWTH PROMPT

This week pretend you are Gentleness as if Gentleness was a person and for 5 minutes write as fast as you can starting with...

♥ ♥

"Don't ever ask me to..."

_____

_____

_____

_____

_____

_____

_____

_____

_____

_____

_____

_____

_____

63 DAYS OF GRATITUDE

THIS WEEK'S MEMORY VERSE

"And we have known and believed the love that God has for us. God is love, and he who abides in love abides in God, and God in him."
1 John 4:16

ONE THING THAT ANNOYED/FRUSTRATED ME TODAY...

_____

_____

_____

_____

_____

_____

GOD, THANK YOU THAT...

_____

_____

_____

_____

_____

_____

SPIRITUAL GROWTH PROMPT

This week pretend you are Gentleness as if Gentleness was a person and for 5 minutes write as fast as you can starting with...

———————— ♥ ♥ ————————

"When I'm filled with joy I tend to..."

_____

_____

_____

_____

_____

_____

_____

_____

_____

_____

_____

_____

_____

63 DAYS OF GRATITUDE

THIS WEEK'S MEMORY VERSE

"And we have known and believed the love that God has for us. God is love, and he who abides in love abides in God, and God in him."
1 John 4:16

ONE THING THAT ANNOYED/FRUSTRATED ME TODAY...

_____

_____

_____

_____

_____

_____

GOD, THANK YOU THAT...

_____

_____

_____

_____

_____

_____

SPIRITUAL GROWTH PROMPT

This week pretend you are Gentleness as if Gentleness was a person and
for 5 minutes write as fast as you can starting with...

❤ ❤

"People really don't like when I..."

_____

_____

_____

_____

_____

_____

_____

_____

_____

_____

_____

_____

_____

TIME TO REFLECT
FIRST...DO YOU SEE ANY PATTERNS IN YOUR WRITING?

SECOND...WHAT ARE YOU MOST GRATEFUL FOR THIS WEEK?

WEEK 9

"Finally, Brethren, whatever things are true, whatever things, are noble, whatever things are just, whatever things are pure, whatever things are lovely, whatever things are of good report, if there is any virtue, and if there is anything praiseworthy, meditate on these things."
Philippians 4:8

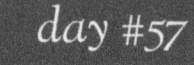

63 DAYS OF GRATITUDE
THIS WEEK'S MEMORY VERSE

"Finally, Brethren, whatever things are true, whatever things, are noble, whatever things are just, whatever things are pure, whatever things are lovely, whatever things are of good report, if there is any virtue, and if there is anything praiseworthy, meditate on these things."
Philippians 4:8

ONE THING THAT ANNOYED/FRUSTRATED ME TODAY...

_____

_____

_____

_____

_____

_____

GOD, THANK YOU THAT...

_____

_____

_____

_____

_____

_____

SPIRITUAL GROWTH PROMPT

This week pretend you are Self Control as if Self Control was a person
and for 5 minutes write as fast as you can starting with...

"It's easy for me to..."

_____

_____

_____

_____

_____

_____

_____

_____

_____

_____

_____

_____

_____

_____

_____

_____

63 DAYS OF GRATITUDE

THIS WEEK'S MEMORY VERSE

"Finally, Brethren, whatever things are true, whatever things, are noble, whatever things are just, whatever things are pure, whatever things are lovely, whatever things are of good report, if there is any virtue, and if there is anything praiseworthy, meditate on these things."
Philippians 4:8

ONE THING THAT ANNOYED/FRUSTRATED ME TODAY...

_____

_____

_____

_____

_____

_____

GOD, THANK YOU THAT...

_____

_____

_____

_____

_____

_____

This week pretend you are Self Control as if Self Control was a person and for 5 minutes write as fast as you can starting with...

♥ ♥

"It's difficult for me to..."

_____

_____

_____

_____

_____

_____

_____

_____

_____

_____

_____

_____

_____

_____

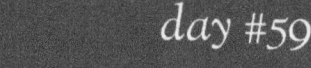

63 DAYS OF GRATITUDE
THIS WEEK'S MEMORY VERSE

"Finally, Brethren, whatever things are true, whatever things, are noble, whatever things are just, whatever things are pure, whatever things are lovely, whatever things are of good report, if there is any virtue, and if there is anything praiseworthy, meditate on these things."
Philippians 4:8

ONE THING THAT ANNOYED/FRUSTRATED ME TODAY...

_____
_____
_____
_____
_____
_____

GOD, THANK YOU THAT...

_____
_____
_____
_____
_____
_____

SPIRITUAL GROWTH PROMPT

This week pretend you are Self Control as if Self Control was a person
and for 5 minutes write as fast as you can starting with...

♥ ♥

"Don't tell anyone, but I..."

_____

_____

_____

_____

_____

_____

_____

_____

_____

_____

_____

_____

_____

63 DAYS OF GRATITUDE
THIS WEEK'S MEMORY VERSE

"Finally, Brethren, whatever things are true, whatever things, are noble, whatever things are just, whatever things are pure, whatever things are lovely, whatever things are of good report, if there is any virtue, and if there is anything praiseworthy, meditate on these things."
Philippians 4:8

ONE THING THAT ANNOYED/FRUSTRATED ME TODAY...

_____

_____

_____

_____

_____

_____

GOD, THANK YOU THAT...

_____

_____

_____

_____

_____

SPIRITUAL GROWTH PROMPT

This week pretend you are Self Control as if Self Control was a person
and for 5 minutes write as fast as you can starting with...

❤ ❤

"When people describe me, they usually talk about my..."

_____

_____

_____

_____

_____

_____

_____

_____

_____

_____

_____

_____

_____

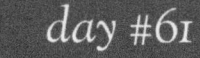

day #61
63 DAYS OF GRATITUDE
THIS WEEK'S MEMORY VERSE

"Finally, Brethren, whatever things are true, whatever things, are noble, whatever things are just, whatever things are pure, whatever things are lovely, whatever things are of good report, if there is any virtue, and if there is anything praiseworthy, meditate on these things."
Philippians 4:8

ONE THING THAT ANNOYED/FRUSTRATED ME TODAY...

_____

_____

_____

_____

_____

_____

GOD, THANK YOU THAT...

_____

_____

_____

_____

_____

_____

SPIRITUAL GROWTH PROMPT

This week pretend you are Self Control as if Self Control was a person
and for 5 minutes write as fast as you can starting with...

♥ ♥

"I look forward to the day when..."

day #62

63 DAYS OF GRATITUDE
THIS WEEK'S MEMORY VERSE

"Finally, Brethren, whatever things are true, whatever things, are noble, whatever things are just, whatever things are pure, whatever things are lovely, whatever things are of good report, if there is any virtue, and if there is anything praiseworthy, meditate on these things."
Philippians 4:8

ONE THING THAT ANNOYED/FRUSTRATED ME TODAY...

_____
_____
_____
_____
_____
_____

GOD, THANK YOU THAT...

_____
_____
_____
_____
_____
_____

SPIRITUAL GROWTH PROMPT

This week pretend you are Self Control as if Self Control was a person
and for 5 minutes write as fast as you can starting with...

❤ ❤

"I doubt that anyone can relate to this, but..."

_____

_____

_____

_____

_____

_____

_____

_____

_____

_____

_____

_____

_____

_____

63 DAYS OF GRATITUDE
THIS WEEK'S MEMORY VERSE

"Finally, Brethren, whatever things are true, whatever things, are noble, whatever things are just, whatever things are pure, whatever things are lovely, whatever things are of good report, if there is any virtue, and if there is anything praiseworthy, meditate on these things."
Philippians 4:8

ONE THING THAT ANNOYED/FRUSTRATED ME TODAY...

_____

_____

_____

_____

_____

_____

GOD, THANK YOU THAT...

_____

_____

_____

_____

_____

SPIRITUAL GROWTH PROMPT

This week pretend you are Self Control as if Self Control was a person and for 5 minutes write as fast as you can starting with...

♥ ♥

"I'm looking for..."

_____

_____

_____

_____

_____

_____

_____

_____

_____

_____

_____

_____

_____

TIME TO REFLECT
FIRST...DO YOU SEE ANY PATTERNS IN YOUR WRITING?

SECOND...WHAT ARE YOU MOST GRATEFUL FOR THIS WEEK?